HOPE & HELP FOR VIDEO GAME, TV & INTERNET "ADDICTION"

MARK SHAW

Hope and Help for Video Game, TV & Internet Addiction
©2008 by Mark Shaw

No part of this book may be reproduced by any means without written consent of the publisher, except for brief quotes used in reviews written specifically for use in a magazine or newspaper.

All Scripture references taken from *The Holy Bible: English Standard Version*, Wheaton: Standard Bible Society, 2001, unless otherwise noted.

Cover design by Melanie Schmidt

Printed in the United States of America

Published by FOCUS PUBLISHING, Inc.
All Rights Reserved

HOPE & HELP FOR VIDEO GAME, TV & INTERNET ADDICTION

"I just conquered a dungeon owned by Orcs and now my reputation is higher so I can buy more items!" exclaims Andrew with glee to his young wife, Rebekah. "I'm getting closer to defeating the whole continent!" he explains.

Ignoring him, Rebekah pleads, "Andrew, I am exhausted. Will you please come to bed with me tonight? You know that expecting mothers need more rest . . . it's best for the baby."

"Rebekah, will you get off my back? I'm not hurting anyone. At least I don't go out drinking with my friends like your 'good for nothing' brother. You can go to bed by yourself 'cause I'm not doing anything wrong."

"You are 'not doing anything' that's for sure," Rebekah mocks back with tears welling in her eyes. As her hands glide coaxingly across her rounded belly, she despairs, "I sure didn't know I was marrying a video game addict."

An Increasing Problem

Ever since the emergence of the very first video game, called "Pong," the progression of technology and sophistication in the video game industry has been ever increasing. Internet and home entertainment system games are becoming so realistic that some people prefer to "live in the fantasy world" of their game rather than deal with a drab, real-life existence. Via an internet "virtual" world game, one man created an imaginary persona, got an imaginary job, met an imaginary female, married her in the imaginary "virtual" internet world, and ended up divorcing his real life wife several months later. He had determined that his female friend who created the imaginary character that married him was a better friend and "virtual" spouse than his legal wife. Unfortunately, his story is not all that unusual as many people who "meet" in the "virtual" world of fantasy plan trips to meet each other in real life.

Millions of children and adults play internet games from cards to fantasy, role playing games and home entertainment games of a wide variety for hours at a time. One gamer admits to me he plays nearly 8 hours per day and 10 to 12 hours on Saturdays and Sundays when he is off from work. In one week, that is an estimated 60 hours. For this reason, the secular world is beginning to label excessive gaming as an "addiction", but is it really an "addiction"? Gamers love playing because in the virtual world you do not gain weight, can quit your job if you are unhappy, and can meet millions of so-called "interesting" people. Video-gaming is a big business and it is escalating rapidly in popularity. Christians who struggle with the temptation to play games to the neglect of their God-given responsibilities must understand the dangers of excessive gaming in terms of biblical truth. In this booklet, the issue of excessive video game playing to the neglect of one's responsibilities is addressed as a sin issue rather than as an "addiction" because there is real hope and help with a Christian and biblical approach.

A "Virtual" World of Games

There is no way to define video gaming comprehensively. It is too big and there are too many varieties of games to mention in this booklet. The focus of this booklet is not to develop a comprehensive list of games that are acceptable to play and games that may be unacceptable because of sinful content. However, it is important to explain that many video and internet games are blatantly sinful.

Many video and internet games encourage your fictional character to commit sins ranging from the murder of innocent persons to sexual immorality. In one video game, the player breaks the law by driving a car recklessly over the speed limit while receiving points for running over innocent bystanders. Blood spews from the dead bodies and points are awarded to the player. Two studies found that playing violent video games "can increase a person's aggressive thoughts, feelings, and behaviors both in laboratory settings and in actual life."[1] The video game player may learn to identify with the aggressor and act out those feelings of aggression and power in real life. Young people are especially prone to such influence. The Bible warns us of the power of the influence of others: **"Do not be deceived: 'Bad company ruins good morals.'"**[2] Are you inviting the influence of "bad company" into your home for hours at a time if you allow your child or loved one to play violent video and internet games, or watch these things on TV?

Sadly, violence is not all you have to be concerned with regarding TV, video and internet games. One gamer informed me that in a home video game, a player can access a "secret room" where he can have "cybersex" with a fictional prostitute with visual effects. Because this portion of the game requires a special password and secret access, the video game's rating may deceive parents into thinking that the game is appropriate for younger players because the "secret" content is not considered by the raters of the game. In other words, parents may purchase a game with a rating that indicates it is appropriate for teenagers yet the "secret" content, if accounted for, would cause the game to be rated for adult players only. Even with an adult rating, the content is sinful as it promotes sexual immorality and impure thoughts of lust. Matthew 5:27-28 states: **"You have heard that it was said, 'You shall not commit adultery.' But I say to you that everyone who looks at a woman with lustful intent has already committed adultery with her in his heart."**

Still other video games promote sexual themes, show nudity of fictional characters (Ephesians 5:3), promote the excessive consumption of alcohol (Ephesians 5:18), promote the consumption of illegal drugs (Romans 13:1-2), and

---

[1] http://www.apa.org/releases/videogames.html provides a brief synopsis of these two studies.
[2] Unless otherwise noted, all verses excerpted from *The Holy Bible: English standard version*. 2001 (electronic ed.). Good News Publishers: Wheaton.

promote profanity (Ephesians 5:4). Christians who play these fictional games are promoting evil and allowing evil to be placed before their eyes. It is not a mindless escape, but a powerful influence that calls "good" what God calls "evil" and Christians are to **"abstain from every form of evil"** according to I Thessalonians 5:22. It is not "innocent fun" but a promotion of evil and sin for which our precious Savior, the Lord Jesus, gave His life upon the cross at Calvary.

Do not be deceived, numerous video and internet games promote sin. I know of at least twenty games that promote violent crimes, sexual immorality, profanity, excessive consumption of alcohol, or the use of illegal drugs. This is true on television programs and today's popular movies as well. Even in a fictional world, sin is still sin. Just because it is portrayed in a "cartoon-like" or comic book manner, these sins are not minimized before God, to whom we must all give an account of our thoughts, words, and actions. Those thoughts and actions in "cyberspace" will be judged by a Righteous God because a real person is thinking the thoughts. At the very least, many cyber games promote living a fictitious life through a created, fictional character where one can commit adultery and murder without consequences, but God is not mocked as He sees and knows all things.

If you are a Christian, you should be able to discern which games promote sinful activities such as sexual immorality, sensuality, drunkenness, idolatry, envy, murder, and greed. If you cannot discern whether the game you are playing is sinful, ask a trusted, mature Christian friend to watch you play and evaluate it biblically for you. If your friend determines the game to be sinful through a biblical evaluation, then you ought to pray to the Lord, confess playing it as sin, and stop playing the game so you can obtain forgiveness and mercy from the Lord as Proverbs 28:13 states: **"Whoever conceals his transgressions will not prosper, but he who confesses and forsakes them will obtain mercy."**

Some gamers spend hard-earned cash on a variety of internet games ranging from fantasy role playing games to games that mimic real life for the user who creates his/her own persona that "exists" in a fantasy world. For some players, these fantasy worlds are more satisfying than real life because they develop cyber-relationships with other gamers from all over the world and "experience" activities that could not otherwise be experienced except in a cyber-world. Money spent on video games ranges from the hundreds to thousands of dollars for the majority of participants, though many of them do not monitor themselves by keeping record of their spending.

Some internet gamers are tempted to meet other internet gamers who live in far away and exotic places. For example, it may be exciting for a person in Mobile, Alabama, to play an internet game with someone in Salem, Oregon, or Japan or Australia. Quite often, an internet gamer "feels closer" to his internet and cyber "friends" than to his friends and family in real life. How sad! The temptation for internet gamers is to take an exotic trip to one of these far away places to meet this cyber friend in real life. When those of the opposite sex meet in this type of rendezvous, you can imagine that the temptation to commit sexual sin is powerful. As you can see, cyber relationships and meetings are very dangerous to one's physical well-being and especially to one's spiritual well-being.

Motivation

Escape, pleasure, and love of control are often the primary reasons a gamer plays excessively. Gaming offers people an "escape" from the rigors of living in a fallen, selfish, and sinful world. Gaming feeds an "escapism" mentality that offers the player a sense of control and pleasure. Gaming is safe, fun, temporarily satisfying, challenging, stimulating, and offers false relationships that seem realistic among the game players. Because society often promotes financial wealth, discontentment, selfishness, and isolationism, internet and video gaming offers the player a fantasy world of wealth, contentment, and "meaningful" relationships that are actually half-truths and deceptions. When gamers leave the imaginary world of gaming, the reality of a fallen world and all of its emptiness awaits them. Television, video and internet games provide a temporarily effective means of escape from trials, relational problems, bills, stressors, and the like.

Herein lies the real problem for family members and friends of an "addicted" video gamer. How can someone help a gamer stop playing the video games that he loves but are hindering the gamer from experiencing a closer relationship with God and others? How does anyone help a gamer who enjoys this type of effective escapism from the harsh realities of the world and does not wish to stop playing? What can be done and what should be done to help a gamer who does not see the dangers of excessive playing?

The deceptiveness of gaming is that the person believes it to be a "personal choice" only affecting oneself; however, knowing the truth of the Bible exposes the pitiful lies of the world for Christians. What is occurring between Andrew and Rebekah in the introduction is being repeated many times over in the world since excessive gaming can have a greater damaging impact on marriages, families, churches, and friendships than one may realize. Nowhere in the Bible will you find an eleventh commandment condemning video game playing: "Thou shalt not play internet or video games." Since that statement or commandment is not in the Bible, some people may wonder, "Is excessive video game playing a sin?"

This question will be answered in the following pages. As you read further, you will find a biblical approach to understanding this issue from a spiritual perspective. In addition, you will find hope and help for addressing this deceptive problem biblically in order to bring about real change that glorifies God. Hope for real change only comes by a proper understanding of biblical truth that is only offered by the illuminating power of the Holy Spirit. In other words, begin by praying that the Holy Spirit will lead you and open the eyes of your heart—of your understanding—with regard to excessive video and internet game playing.

Is Video Game Playing a Sin?

Unfortunately, sin is deceptive and not well understood by many Christians today. Sin is any thought, word, or action that is contrary to the Word of God. Sin offends a Holy God. Sin is never a "mistake" and always involves the human will. Because God is perfectly just, He holds sinners responsible for their sins and promises to punish unrepentant, unwilling, and unbelieving sinners with an eternal destination in Hell. If you do not like that previous statement, you will have to address the matter with God Himself who is the Creator of all things. As Creator, God is the Owner of all things, including you and me.

There are two types of sin. The first type of sin is called a sin of commission because it involves a transgression of one of God's laws. These types of sins include adultery, stealing, lying, and drunkenness. In these sinful acts, the sinner is committing a sin by *doing* something wrong that displeases God. It is clear because it is an action that is visible. It is a sin of *doing*.

The second type of sin is called a sin of omission, and this is the category of sin that most video and internet gaming situations fall under. Sins of omission are those that involve not being or doing what God requires.[3] These types of sins include *not* loving one's wife as Christ loves the Church, not honoring one's husband, not serving one another, not loving one another, not parenting and teaching one's children, and not working hard at one's job as unto the Lord. These sins are hard to address in the context of a biblical counseling session or in a marriage relationship because neglecting to do the things God requires is *not* often clearly identifiable. These sins of "*not doing*" are often not pointed out by counselors and family members.

These sins of omission, although not easily detectable at first, show up in a huge way over time. For example, a failure

---

[3] Taken from "Kids' Quest Catechism Club," Great Commission Publications Inc, Suwanee, GA, 2003.

to be a good steward of one's money and resources may take several months to detect until one nears bankruptcy. In like manner, a video game "addiction" by a husband causes him to neglect spending time with his wife as he fails to love her as Christ loves the Church. In time, the frustrated wife may file for divorce because she is tired of living with a selfish man who enjoys video entertainment more than he does spending quality time with his spouse.

Many video gamers involved in this type of sin of omission think they are "not hurting anyone else." This is a lie! Sins of omission hurt the gamer and those relationships that the gamer holds dear. Sins of omission cannot be hidden from God who sees all things and knows all things, including the fact that these sins do indeed harm other people. Even so-called "little sins" like dishonoring a parent, lusting after a pornographic image, or playing hours of self-focused video entertainment *seem* to be small but really cause the sinner to be separated from a healthy relationship with God and loved ones.

In reality, no sin is "little;" all sin has consequences that affect the sinner's relationship with God and others. For example, when the gamer feels separated from God, the Lord did not leave or disappear from the gamer though the sinner mistakenly *thinks* that He does! It is the sinner who walks down his own path and leaves God instead of walking down God's path with God. It is very easy to live and walk in the passions of one's flesh rather than be led by the Holy Spirit of God. It is very easy to think that the Lord has abandoned you when you are ensnared to sin, but He has not left you nor forsaken you if you are indeed His child.[4]

Isn't it odd that Christians – who have experienced the wonderful and immeasurable gift of forgiveness from all sins – often hate to admit that they still struggle with the temptation to sin? Christ Jesus died on the cross for all Christians' sins including those of omission – no matter how heinous those sins are. Jesus was buried and raised from the dead, and

---

[4] Hebrews 13:5 and II Corinthians 4:9.

because He lives, the Christian now lives his life as one who has been forgiven and is grateful for the free gift of salvation. This state of being reckoned as righteous in God's eyes does not mean that Christians will not commit any further sins, or struggle with sins of omission, because Christians still have a sinful nature called "the flesh" in the Bible.

The Deceptive Power of Sin

The flesh – which includes the habits of both thought and behavior – battles the Christian's new desire to be led by the Holy Spirit that indwells them. When you forget that you are in spiritual warfare against your own flesh, it is easy to continue walking according to the flesh even after repentance and conversion.[5] Don't forget that the Holy Spirit dwells inside of you to help you in this battle.

You may not have realized that your thoughts can be habitual. Much research is being conducted today to study the brain and its impact upon behavior. Actions that seem "compulsive" because they are so automatic are really not compulsive at all but are "habitual." Habits form by repetition. If you have ever ridden a bike, you know that when you first rode that bike you were in danger of crashing at any moment. However, as you practiced day after day, you became so proficient at riding a bike that you could travel rather efficiently at high speeds and even do tricks on your bike. You developed the habit of riding the bike safely, and you could even do so today if necessary. Even though dormant for years, habits are deeply imbedded in your flesh. Remember the coined phrase, "just like riding a bike"? That phrase implies that no one ever forgets how to ride a bike because it is a learned habit. Bad habits and poor thinking patterns are very powerful modes of operation for our sinful flesh.

Our thinking processes are habitual, but the problem is that our thoughts as non-Christians were continually focused upon pleasing ourselves. Now, as Christians, we often go

---

[5] Ephesians 5:1-21 and I Corinthians 10:1-14.

back to that way of habitual thinking (pleasing ourselves) when the Lord calls us to think about how we can please Him and others. It is a difficult struggle to be a Christian because it is unnatural to our minds and bodies. The power of the fruitful Christian life comes from the Holy Spirit working in conjunction with the Word of Truth (the Bible). You must be intentional in your Christian walk and purposeful with what you choose to think about according to Colossians 3:1-2: **"If then you have been raised with Christ, seek the things that are above, where Christ is, seated at the right hand of God. Set your minds on things that are above, not on things that are on earth."**

The key now is for you to replace your habitual thoughts of pleasing yourself with new thoughts that come from the Word of God alone. These are the thoughts that please God. The extent to which you *intentionally* put the Word of God into your mind is the extent to which the Holy Spirit can empower you. The two are strongly interrelated Another clear command found in Scripture regarding our thoughts can be found in Philippians 4:8: **"Finally, brothers, whatever is true, whatever is honorable, whatever is just, whatever is pure, whatever is lovely, whatever is commendable, if there is any excellence, if there is anything worthy of praise, think about these things."**

When you watch TV, play video games, or enter a "virtual" internet world for hours at a time, you are not being intentional with your mind. You are "amusing" yourself. The word "amuse" means to "go without thinking" and it is used to describe "amusement parks" and similar entertainment modalities. To "go without thinking" is an escape that is primarily designed to please yourself and neglect your responsibilities. At its root, it is selfish and a sin issue. You must learn to be intentional in your thinking and intentional regarding the best use of your time.

The case for biblical hope and help begins with one primary assumption. The Word of God is absolute, authoritative, and sufficient. 2 Timothy 3:16-17 states: **"All**

Scripture is breathed out by God and profitable for teaching, for reproof, for correction, and for training in righteousness, that the man of God may be competent, equipped for every good work." Whatever subject that Scripture speaks to must be accepted as the *divine opinion*. It cannot be set aside in favor of tolerance and relevancy in an ever-changing society with ever-changing moral values. It must be accepted as inarguable fact. Mankind must be viewed as responsible in reference to this truth. Acting upon God's Word as absolute and sufficient truth runs counter to the world's system of thinking, which paints gamers as "compulsive" and "out of control." Gaming is "habitual" not "compulsive" and the Word of God holds mankind responsible for sin.

Excessive video gaming is very often a sin of omission. Gaming is an action, but the thinking errors and motives of the heart that lead to gaming are sinful. God hates sin because it destroys the sinner. God is not a "cosmic killjoy" in heaven who wants to take away a gamer's fun! Instead, God is loving and good and knows that sinful gaming seriously harms the gamer and often the gamer's loved ones. Sin is destructive and the excessive video gamer will be destroyed if not for the love of God.

God's Goodness and Why He Hates Sin

What does all of this have to do with gaming? Often, unrepentant and unwilling gamers say, "Playing a virtual game is not a sin. It's not a real sin like murder, adultery, or stealing. Where in the Bible does it say that playing a video game of any sort is a sin?" Again, the sin is not what you are doing when you are playing a video game. The sin is what you are *failing* to do while you play the video game. Excessive gaming leads to a failure of God-given, biblical responsibilities in a variety of areas and relationships. There are consequences of sins of commission, and there are consequences of sins of omission. Furthermore, the heart issues driving someone to play video games excessively can be evaluated biblically since the Bible has much to say about the heart of mankind.

Are you willing to view your excessive video gaming as sinful in God's eyes because of your failure to fulfill your God-given responsibilities to serve, love, and honor others? If so, keep reading and implement some of the suggestions mentioned in this booklet. If not, then I encourage you to read further with an open mind to the Holy Spirit's conviction. Be sensitive and open to what God's Word says about sin, pride, and stewardship. God wants to keep you from sin because He knows that sin separates you from Him and those persons in your life who love you most. Sin primarily hurts you and the Lord knows it. His laws and Word are designed to protect you from the destruction of sin. He commands you to obey Him because He loves you and desires to protect you. His authority over you as Creator is good and loving. It is not threatening. Satan tries to tell people that God cannot be both loving and authoritative over you. Satan used the same lie in the Garden of Eden with Adam and Eve; it worked because mankind wants to believe that he can be his own god and rule his life better than his Creator God – better than his Owner.

Excessive video gaming and neglecting one's God-given responsibilities will ultimately catch up with you. You may enjoy your games now and the imaginary pleasures and relationships you are developing, but you will eventually end up alone because sin separates the sinner from God and loved ones. Sin leads a person away from others and into a world of isolation – a world of self-seeking, self-absorbed pleasure. These are the inevitable results of sinful behavior.

Sins of omission set the sinner up as king of his own domain; some other people will join the sinner in that domain for awhile, but not for very long. Eventually, people see through the selfishness of the sinner and grow weary of having a one-sided relationship. Loved ones feel as though they are doing all of the "giving" with the sinner of omission doing all of the "taking." Ultimately, the video gamer will find himself alone and wondering why he has been "abandoned." He or she may develop a "victim mentality" that causes him to wonder, "What's the big deal and why did you abandon me?"

Several video gamers have said to themselves, "Why am I all alone? Where did everyone go? Don't they love me?"

Honest Self-Evaluation

Ask yourself: "Am I acting faithfully to God and to my loved ones?" Proverbs 13:15 warns: **"Good understanding gains favor, but the way of the unfaithful is hard."**[6] In other words, when you choose the path of living for yourself rather than living by faith and for the Lord, you end up walking a difficult road full of frustration and trials. Are you living for yourself by playing countless hours of video games? Are you neglecting some of your primary relationships including your relationship with the Lord? Are you doing all things to the glory of God?[7]

Take just a moment now to reflect upon ways you may be failing God and/or those persons with whom you have primary relationships (spouse, children, boss, co-workers, extended family members, friends, and members of your church). Make a list of ways you have failed them and ask them to review your list and add to it anything that you may not have known or remembered. Once they finish, take the list and ask for forgiveness from the Lord and from them directly. Then, write out a practical plan of repentance for each item listed. Ask your loved one to help you with that plan and to rank the items in terms of most important to least important. Finally, implement at least one of those repentance items each week by starting with the most important item first.

Now, before we move on, take just a moment to reflect upon the Lord's goodness to you in the sacrifice of His only begotten Son. Ask the Lord to change your heart's desire for excessive TV or video gaming into a desire to love and honor God by the power of the Holy Spirit. Read and meditate (think on) these verses now to remind yourself of the goodness of

---

[6] *The New King James Version*. 1996, c1982. Thomas Nelson: Nashville.
[7] I Corinthians 10:31.

God: John 3:16, Romans 5:8, Ephesians 2:4, 2 Thessalonians 2:16-17, 1 John 3:1, and 1 John 4:9-10. A life lived for God's glory rather than selfish pleasures is fulfilling and fruitful. It is a better life than any man-made, "virtual world" can offer. To add icing to the cake, the Christian can look forward instead to what heaven offers! A Christian life lived for God is an awesome adventure with a bright, eternal future.

Three Motives of the Video Gamer's Heart

What are the heart issues that drive a gamer to play video games excessively? As already mentioned, three primary reasons a gamer plays excessively are escape, pleasure, and love of control. We will see that these never fully satisfy an insatiable appetite.

Escape

A desire to escape the rigors of a drab, fallen world plagues unbelievers and many Christians who are not living their lives unto the Lord. Even King David once desired to escape in Psalm 55:6-8: **"And I say, 'Oh, that I had wings like a dove! I would fly away and be at rest; yes, I would wander far away; I would lodge in the wilderness; I would hurry to find a shelter from the raging wind and tempest.'"** While King David's desire for escape was due to the treachery of his enemies, the gamer may *think* of his world as treacherous because of living in a fallen world (Genesis 3) and of the consequences of living for self.

To combat the desire to escape from a fallen world and its problems, the gamer must change his thinking from a "victim mentality" which is passive to an "action mentality" which is active. A victim is one who is adversely affected by circumstances and either is (or perceives himself to be) powerless in changing those circumstances. It is very sad to be a victim and every person on the planet has experienced being a victim of someone else's sinful choice(s). For example, if you have ever lost a game to a cheater, then technically you were wronged and "victimized." This type of victimization is minor when compared to sexual and physical abuse but it illustrates the concept of victimization.

If the victim dwells on the event in which he was sinned against, then he or she may never truly heal, never really overcome the event, and thus, may remain a victim forever. Persons who learn to take the wrong and turn it around for good do not remain victims but become *victors* by God's grace and power! That is the redemptive character of God who turns evil into blessing for His children according to Romans 8:28: **"And we know that for those who love God all things work together for good, for those who are called according to his purpose."** God wants His children to view trials and problems through the proper, biblical lenses. God wants His children to see that life's trials are designed to bring them closer to Himself in that relationship, and designed to make them more Christ-like in character.

God gives you the solution to this desire of escape in your heart in I Timothy 6:11-12: **"But as for you, O man of God, flee these things. Pursue righteousness, godliness, faith, love, steadfastness, gentleness. Fight the good fight of the faith. Take hold of the eternal life to which you were called and about which you made the good confession in the presence of many witnesses."** Christians are to flee from the selfish pursuits of the love of excessive video gaming. We are to focus our thoughts upon the gift of eternal life with the Lord rather than upon the temporal pleasures of this world. Christians are to pursue the things of God, which are committing righteous, godly, faithful, loving, steadfast, and gentle acts out of a desire to please the Lord and help others. Do gamers pursue such things or do they pursue activities that fulfill selfish desires?

A gamer often wastes his God-given talents and abilities upon selfish pursuits. If God has given you a spouse and/or children and you are neglecting time that could be spent faithfully and intentionally teaching them, then it is clearly a sin to excessively play games and fail to meet your God-given responsibilities. If God has not given you a spouse or children, He may be calling you to live your life to serve Him by helping those who are less fortunate than you. There are many people in hospitals, nursing homes, orphanages, shelters, and drug treatment centers with whom you could visit, serve, love, and share your faith in Christ. By wasting countless hours in front of a computer screen or television, you are not fulfilling the call of God to be focused upon helping people and you are failing in your God-given purpose to serve Him. Ephesians 2:10 reminds us: **"For we are his workmanship, created in Christ Jesus for good works, which God prepared beforehand, that we should walk in them."**

Pleasure

Similar to a desire for escape, a second motive in a gamer's heart is a desire for pleasure. The gamer may not want to escape from the rigors of this fallen world; rather, the gamer lives his life for sensual, temporary pleasures. As stated before, this desire for pleasure is a focus primarily upon pleasing self rather than pleasing God. While it is true that God does not call everyone to live in little, straw huts, He does want us be focused upon serving and pleasing Him by serving or ministering to others. God may grant us temporary pleasures in this world because He is good and gracious; however, God may also call us to leave our "comfort zone" so that we might serve Him. Seek to serve Him more than you seek to please yourself and you will find mercy.

A person who is driven by feelings and a pursuit of sensual pleasures will never be satisfied and always be frustrated with life. Anger, bitterness, and depression tend to characterize a sensual person's life. A pleasure-driven person becomes purposeless; and therefore becomes useless to God and society. The pleasure-driven person's purpose is in pleasing self, so they move continually from one pleasure to the next. There is no end point in sight for this person.

Ephesians 4:17-24 addresses this problem and its pitfalls and offers real hope for change:

> "Now this I say and testify in the Lord, that you must no longer walk as the Gentiles do, in the futility of their minds. [18] They are darkened in their understanding, alienated from the life of God because of the ignorance that is in them, due to their hardness of heart. [19] They have become callous and have given themselves up to sensuality, greedy to practice every kind of impurity. [20] But that is not the way you learned Christ!— [21] assuming that you have heard about him and were taught in him, as the truth is in Jesus, [22] to put off your old self, which belongs to your former manner of life and is corrupt through deceitful desires, [23] and to be renewed in the spirit of your minds, [24] and to put on the new self, created after the likeness of God in true righteousness and holiness."

As mentioned in Ephesians 4 above, is your "understanding darkened"? Do you feel "alienated," or distanced, from God? Do you have a hard heart toward the Lord or toward your sin? Have you become "callous" to the things of God? If you answer any or all of these questions with a "yes," then you likely have fallen into a lifestyle of "sensuality," or living to please your basest desires. You are not in a good place, but there is hope in Christ.

What you must do is to "put off your old self" including your old way of thinking. In other words, you must stop what you are doing that is primarily sensual and even stop desiring it. You must be "renewed in the spirit of your mind" so that you view what you once loved as something that is now hated. That game that you love to play is an enemy and not a friend because it separates you from the love of God. Your thinking (mind) must change in this regard. Your thinking must become like God's thinking as revealed in His Word. Because all are born in sin and have sinful thinking that follows the world's best ideas, the Bible tells you that your thinking must be "renewed, transformed, and changed" into what the Lord would have it be. Romans 12:2 states: **"Do not be conformed to this world, but be transformed by the renewal of your mind, that by testing you may discern what is the will of God, what is good and acceptable and perfect."**

Once this occurs, you are ready for the "put on" part of the equation which is truly the best part of the transformation process! In the "put on" stage of the process, you get to become the "new creation in Christ"[8] "created after the likeness of God in true righteousness and holiness." In other words, you must "put on" new behaviors that are Christ-like and glorify God. You can "put on" anything you like as long as it meets the criteria of glorifying the Lord. You can do a multitude of things that bring glory to Him. In a sense, you are only limited to your own imagination. Make a list of new behaviors and new pursuits that you can begin to implement in your life. For example, maybe you possess a talent that you could teach at a nursing home or to sick children at a hospital. Ask a loved one to help you to devise this list. Be creative! Then, implement at least one item each week. If you want to concentrate on only one item, then work to implement it in some measure daily for the next three months.

Hard work is the means to implement the "put on" list you have developed. Christians ought to be hard workers out of a thankful heart to God who redeemed them from their fallen state. Honoring God is the least a Christian can do to demonstrate to a dying world that God is loving and forgiving of repentant sinners. The Lord assigned work to mankind before The Fall according to Genesis 2:15: **"The LORD God took the man and put him in the Garden of Eden to work it and keep it."**

Work is an essential element in a Christian approach to life. Mankind finds purpose in Christ when he works and is productive for the glory of God. By excessively watching

---

[8] II Corinthians 5:17.

TV or playing video games, you are failing to work. A strong statement to deter you from this fallen mindset is II Thessalonians 3:10-12: **"For even when we were with you, we would give you this command: If anyone is not willing to work, let him not eat. For we hear that some among you walk in idleness, not busy at work, but busybodies. Now such persons we command and encourage in the Lord Jesus Christ to do their work quietly and to earn their own living."** I Corinthians 10:31 reminds you: **"So, whether you eat or drink, or whatever you do, do all to the glory of God."** Therefore, do your work and your list of "put on's" for God's glory and avoid being driven primarily by pleasure.

Love of Control

In the hearts of all sinful men and women is a desire to be "gods" of their own destinies. It is called "idolatry" in the Bible. Do a word study on "idolatry" and you will find that all idolatrous behaviors are rooted in a desire to please self. In biblical times, God's people would worship false idols (as the pagans did) because they wanted to receive a blessing of money or rain for crops. The "worship" of the false idol was only performed out of a selfish motive for gain, as if the worship would constrain the gods to bless them. Today, many gamers "worship" the idol of living in a "virtual world" with a new identity because it fulfills their desire for control.

By control, a gamer is trusting in self rather than trusting in God to provide for his needs. The gamer thinks he knows better than the Lord and has the audacity to say in his heart, "I can do better than you, Lord. I can have more fun in my fantasy world of games than I can in your created world." That may not be a spoken or outward manifestation but these statements rule the heart of the gamer more often than not. There is a self-reliant attitude that drives the gamer. The Bible repeatedly warns against this type of prideful attitude. For example, Proverbs 3:5-7: **"Trust in the Lord with all your heart, and do not lean on your own understanding. In all your ways acknowledge him, and he will make straight your** paths. Be not wise in your own eyes; fear the LORD, and turn away from evil." Pride is at the root of the love of control. It is pretty clear that God wants us to trust in Him alone and not ourselves or any temporary pleasure.

God is clear in His Word that He desires you to acknowledge that all of life, including riches and wealth, have come by His hand, not your own, and that He is the provider of everything good. Deuteronomy 8:17-20 states:

> "Beware lest you say in your heart, 'My power and the might of my hand have gotten me this wealth.' You shall remember the LORD your God, for it is he who gives you power to get wealth that he may confirm his covenant that he swore to your fathers, as it is this day. And if you forget the LORD your God and go after other gods and serve them and worship them, I solemnly warn you today that you shall surely perish. And if you forget the LORD your God and go after other gods and serve them and worship them, I solemnly warn you today that you shall surely perish. Like the nations that the LORD makes to perish before you, so shall you perish, because you would not obey the voice of the LORD your God."

Do not "go after other gods" which is the idolatry of excessive video gaming! Your false world of internet and "virtual identity" may seem fun and provide a pleasurable diversion in your life, but it will ruin your real relationships and eventually render you an empty existence devoid of a thriving relationship with the Almighty Lord.

In a "virtual" world, the gamer has freedom to do what he wants to do; an ability to create, and demonstrate power in that domain. The gamer will never get fat and can live "virtually" without consequences. It is very appealing and compelling and is akin to being a "god" of that world. It is true that the Lord wants you to be creative and to use your imagination to His glory, but most gamers are playing and living in a "virtual world" for selfish reasons. Ask yourself: "Am I content being a created being who answers to the Creator God or do I prefer living as a 'god' of my own world?" Do not fool yourself: the desire to be "god" of your fantasy world will "spill over" into your real world causing you frustration and anger when situations are out of your control. Since you are a created being, the things in this world are not designed to be in your control. You will get frustrated with the realities of a sinfully fallen world.

Are you content to be a created being and to find your purpose in the Almighty God's plan of redemption for your life? The heart of the gamer may want control because he thinks he "can do better than God" and wants "to do what I want to do." Both of these thoughts are prideful and focused upon pleasing oneself rather than upon pleasing God. God wants the gamer to work hard for His glory at the gamer's God-given job!

Often, a lack of contentment with what God has given us is really an evil heart attitude, proving a lack of faith in our Good God. According to Matthew 15:19-20, Jesus taught: **"For out of the heart come evil thoughts, murder, adultery, sexual immorality, theft, false witness, slander. These are what defile a person."** The motives of your heart are what defile you before the Lord so you must change what you desire by changing your thoughts—not just your actions. You must want what God wants for you and you must learn to be content with what He has provided for you. The Apostle Paul had to learn contentment so the gamer should not think he is any different. Philippians 4:11 states: **"Not that I am speaking of being in need, for I have learned in whatever situation I am to be content."** Contentment is learned by training your thoughts to focus upon the gracious provisions of your Heavenly Father. Are you thankful for what the Lord has given you? Are you content to be a new creation in Christ?

Do you have a desire for more than what God has provided for you? Is your attitude one of discontentment? Living for control and for pleasing ourselves more than God are insatiable desires that frequently result from a desire to be honored, recognized, and respected by others for what we have done in our own power. This prideful attitude fails to honor God or to recognize Him as the great Provider that He is. As you can see, this mindset is very dangerous. One reason God hates the pride that fosters this type of "controlling" attitude is that it ultimately leads to separation, isolation, and destruction for the video gamer.[9]

All to the Glory of God

The primary goal in life is to love and honor God with our thoughts, words, and actions, and to love our neighbors as ourselves. Excessive gaming does not please God because it is most often a sin of omission resulting in a failure to love others.

It is clear that the Bible commands the Christian to have his mind renewed by Scripture. Romans 12:2 states: **"Do not be conformed to this world, but be transformed by the renewal of your mind, that by testing you may discern what is the will of God, what is good and acceptable and perfect."** Let's address how the gamer is to repent in word and action.

Words alone mean very little to the loved one of an excessive internet gamer because of the lies and disappointments of the past. Therefore, the gamer must do two things: 1) speak words of repentance and 2) demonstrate repentance is taking place by his or her actions. In other words, now, he must "walk the talk." This action aspect of repentance is difficult without some type of accountability partner.

The gamer must get a trusted Christian friend who will commit to pray for them. In addition, the trusted Christian friend is expected to take daily phone calls from the gamer as a type of "check in" for daily accountability. "How are you doing?" is a fine question but the tough questions should be asked, too, during this daily phone call. The trusted Christian

---

[9] Proverbs 6:17, Proverbs 8:13, and Psalm 101:5.

friend is to ask the gamer what he is primarily thinking about today, what Scriptures have been meditated upon and read, and if the gamer has been actively participating in any "time wasting" activities today.

The gamer is responsible for being truthful and forthright in this conversation. No one can force him into this honesty, however, here is a wonderful truth of the Bible – it is the power of the Holy Spirit that causes the Christian gamer to will and to do the right things. Philippians 2:13 states: **"For it is God who works in you, both to will and to work for his good pleasure."**

Again, the primary goal of all Christians must be to please God in all things as stated in I Corinthians 10:31: **"So, whether you eat or drink, or whatever you do, do all to the glory of God."** Where is God in your life right now? Do you have a God-centered mindset or a self-centered mindset? Are you content with what the Lord has given you? God requires radical obedience but always empowers Christians to implement His commands. You can do this because He can do this through you. He is the God of the Universe.

A Practical Plan of Action

In several verses of the Bible, God commands His people to be "doers" of the Word and not just "hearers" only. What is your plan of action for overcoming your excessive gaming habits? I have alluded to some things that you should do earlier in this booklet, but let's develop a biblically based, practical plan to implement right away.

1. Find a trusted Christian friend to hold you accountable daily. Change occurs best when a gamer is held accountable by a tangible person. The word "tangible" is used because some gamers want to say, "God holds me accountable." While that is a true statement, gamers need someone that is "tangible" and can be seen, heard, and touched. The Lord works through people to demonstrate His loving kindness, so ask a trusted Christian friend to commit to do the things discussed earlier in this booklet. It is recommended that you get a same-sex person to fulfill this role. It is preferable that this same-sex person be an older person and a more mature Christian if possible. Also, it is recommended that it not be a spouse so that you will have an additional person to hold you accountable. A spouse is a wonderful blessing from the Lord to help you in accountability, but you also need someone else.

2. **Journal the time you spend each day thinking about gaming-related activities and thinking about the Lord.** Keep a 3 x 5 index card in your pocket or purse so you can write down the time spent on each activity periodically throughout your day. By "gaming-related activities," I mean anything that is entertaining and meant to give you pleasure apart from pleasing the Lord. This may include a variety of activities so if you are not sure, write it down on your card and ask your trusted Christian friend to review it with you. Analyze your activities that are "amusement" rather than intentional activities. Are more hours spent in "amusement" or in an intentional, Christian mindset?

3. **Get involved in serving others in some capacity.** Hopefully, you are working to earn an honest living, but working is not enough according to Ephesians 4:28: **"Let the thief no longer steal, but rather let him labor, doing honest work with his own hands, so that he may have something to share with anyone in need."** In a way, you have been operating as a "thief" by squandering your God-given abilities and time upon pleasing yourself. Now, it is time to "share with anyone in need" so that means you can give your *time* to a charitable cause of your choice. Work at a homeless mission, visit a nursing home, volunteer to set up chairs at your church, or do whatever the Lord has made you passionate about in a service-type of role in any service organization. It really does not matter because the verse says "anyone in need" and there is no shortage of needs in this world. The majority of these activities (and many more) are suitable "put on" behaviors for you because they serve others and honor the Lord.

4. Read and study your Bible daily. Read passages dealing with the stewardship of your time and abilities. If you are not sure where those are, ask your pastor, deacon or elder, biblical counselor, or mature Christian friend to help you learn how to study the Bible. Study topics in the Bible that interest you and are current struggles for you. Pick out a verse or two to memorize that specifically deal with your particular struggles so that it is relevant to you. God wants you to intentionally focus your thoughts upon Him and transform your thinking into Godly thinking. The only way to do this is by faithful and intentional Bible study.

5. Become intentional in your walk with the Lord. Get up early each day. Spend the first moments of your day with the Lord in prayer and Bible study. A mindset that is intentional is active, and not passive. Be on the offensive against this world and the devil. Plan ahead to do what is right in the sight of God[10] and seek to please Him first.

Conclusion

While not physically addictive, excessive video gaming is considered to be a type of "addiction" because of the destruction that gaming behaviors can cause. It simply does not make sense to play hours of video games to those who are "non-gamers;" therefore, many of them label it as an "addiction" rather than as a "sin problem." More devastating than the behaviors of excessive gaming are the *thoughts* of the gamer: sinfully desiring an escape, pleasure, power, and the love of control to the neglect of fulfilling God-given responsibilities. These heart desires lead one to experience the temporal pleasures of excessive gaming because eternity is often not in the mind of the gamer. Worldly thinking does not embrace the idea of serving God, working hard, and giving to others. Instead, worldly thinking encourages selfishness, discontentment, and unhappiness.

---

[10] Romans 12:17.

The Bible promotes a radically different view of life: You should seek to please your Lord and Savior with a thankful heart that has received a free gift of eternal life. When you serve your Lord by serving others and have an obedient lifestyle, you will reap blessings and overcome your gaming habits. Although your primary goal is not to receive blessings, obedience to your Creator, Savior, and Sustainer will produce an abundance of blessings and fruit in your life because your mindset changes from a worldly focus into a Christ-like focus. The fruit that manifests is "love, joy, peace, patience, kindness, goodness, faithfulness, gentleness, and self-control."[11] Don't you want to abundantly experience these things in your life? Take a moment to re-read each one of these fruit of the Christian life slowly right now and ask yourself to what extent you possess each one of them.

When you seek to glorify God in every area of your life, you will strive to serve others who are often more needy than you. Although the Christian life is hard work, it is designed to bring glory to God and to send a Gospel message of grace, mercy, and love to the world. Is that the goal in your life? Is your goal to please God? If you obey the Word of God by loving and serving others in ways that please Him, your life will be purposeful, a blessing to others, and a blessing to you as you will overcome your gaming habits.

God enables all Christians to obey His commands by the power of the Holy Spirit working in conjunction with His Word of Truth. Even though gaming will not go away in this age, the Christian who struggles with gaming can learn to re-focus his thoughts upon the things of God that are eternal and fulfilling both in this life and in the everlasting life to come. Our merciful God forgives all of your sins that are confessed and forsaken by His grace alone, and through your faith in Christ alone according to I John 1:9-10: **"If we confess our sins, he is faithful and just to forgive us our sins and to cleanse us from all unrighteousness. If we say we have not sinned, we make him a liar, and his word is not in us."**

---

[11] Galatians 5:22-23.

It is "good news" to know that you have a Divine Advocate in Jesus Christ your Lord and Savior. II John 2:1 says: **"My little children, I am writing these things to you so that you may not sin. But if anyone does sin, we have an advocate with the Father, Jesus Christ the righteous."** Commit your life to Him today by serving His people and those that are lost and without hope because they do not know the risen Savior, Christ Jesus. Live your life for His glory by serving others and you will find real fulfillment in a fallen world as I Peter 4:10-11 states: **"As each has received a gift, use it to serve one another, as good stewards of God's varied grace: whoever speaks, as one who speaks oracles of God; whoever serves, as one who serves by the strength that God supplies—in order that in everything God may be glorified through Jesus Christ. To him belong glory and dominion forever and ever. Amen."**

APPENDIX
PRACTICAL HELPS

Focus your thoughts upon the gift of eternal life with the Lord rather than upon the temporal pleasures of this world.

1. Scriptures on which to meditate about your salvation and God's goodness to you:

    John 3:16

    Romans 5:8

    Ephesians 2:4

    2 Thessalonians 2:16-17

    1 John 3:1

    1 John 4:9-10

2. Read and review this booklet and write down all Scripture verses listed. Study those and ask a trusted Christian friend to teach you what you do not understand.

Developing a Practical Plan of Action

1. Find a trusted Christian friend to hold you accountable daily. Make a list of three to five persons with their phone numbers to contact to ask if they will consider being your accountability partner.

2. Keep a 3 x 5 index card with you at all times in order to journal the time you spend each day thinking about any "amusement" and video gaming-related activities. Also, document on that card how much time you spend in prayer, Bible reading, meditation, and memorization of Scripture.

3. Get involved in serving others in some capacity. Make a list of activities and places where you can serve. Ask your accountability partner or pastor to help you devise this list if you need help.

4. Read and study your Bible daily. Schedule a specific time slot each day for prayer and Bible study.
5. Become intentional in your walk with the Lord. Plan your day to focus upon pleasing your Savior and designate time to accomplish those goals.

How to Develop and Implement a Confession List

1. Make a list of ways you have failed your primary relationships (spouse, children, boss, co-workers, extended family members, friends, members of your church).
2. Ask them to review your list and add to it anything that you may not have known or remembered.
3. Once they finish, take the list and ask for forgiveness from the Lord and from them directly.
4. Then, write out a practical plan of repentance for each item listed.
5. Ask your loved one to help you with that plan and to rank the items in terms of most important to least important.
6. Finally, implement at least one of those repentance items each week by starting with the most important item first.